Unlocking the Magic of Time

A Kids Book Inspiring Communities Through Financial Growth and Education!

Book 3 of the My First Finance Illustrated Book Series

Written by Ben Hofstetter and Nick Zehrung

New Caney, TX
2023

A book in the Children's Financial Literacy and Learning Path

Library of Congress Control Number: 2023918046

Table of Contents

"We make a living by what we get, but we make a life by what we give."

- Winston Churchill

Chapter 1:

Local Hero:

Building a Brighter Tomorrow by Investing in Your Own Community

For Parents

Key Themes Explored in this chapter:

- In this chapter we discuss the importance of building up our entire community and making it a better place for everyone to live, not just ourselves.

- We show that investing time and money (volunteering and charitable donations) are equally important for helping those around us.

- The concept of a non-profit business is introduced and discussed.

- Several examples are given throughout the chapter showing ways to give back to the community that anyone can do, like cleaning up the local park. "Rising tides lift all boats!"

In Books 1 and 2 of this series we learned about three ways to use our money:

1) We can spend money on things we need or want

2) We can save our money for later (in a wallet or magic piggy bank)

3) We can invest our money by starting our own business, helping a friend start a business, or in many businesses with lots of other people

Investing doesn't always have to be done to make more money!

We can also invest our time, money, and resources into things which make our whole community a better place for everyone!

Investing in our community means using our resources to help others and make a positive impact for the people we share the world with!

It can be as simple as donating toys or clothes that we no longer need to people who could benefit from them!

We could also volunteer our time to help with local community projects, like feeding the homeless or cleaning up a local park!

In previous books we learned that by doing things that provide value to our community we can earn money and make it a better place.

But it's also important to know that we can make a positive impact on our community by helping others without expecting anything in return.

For example, you could help teach a classmate on a subject you are an expert in just because you're friends!

Over the next few pages we'll talk about the difference between adding value and making a positive impact, and why it's important to do both!

Remember when we had our lemonade stand? Our customers were thirsty people who wanted a refreshing drink.

We provided value to them by getting all the supplies, making the drinks, and being available for them to buy from us.

The most important thing to remember about this is that they could have made their own lemonade, but we saved them time and effort. Without us, they would have had to go to the store and do all the work to make the drink. So we provided value to them by doing that for them!

Sometimes there are things that people need, but can't get for some reason.

When we do something to help others who can't get what we're offering in any other way, it's called making a positive impact!

For example, someone might not have the money to pay for our lemonade. But if you give them a glass to cool off on a hot day, even though they can't pay you, you're making a positive impact on your community and that person's life!

Often there are groups of people who are experts at a specific job and they make a positive impact on the community by doing that job. If you give them some of your money to help them accomplish their goals, it's called making a donation!

For example, you might not be able to help every dog that needs a home. But you can donate a few dollars to a local pet shelter that will use it to provide food for a lonely puppy.

By giving money to a group of people who are experts in taking care of many dogs, you're helping the puppy and making a positive impact in your community!

Did you know you can start a special kind of business that makes money to support the community? It's called a non-profit!

Non-profits work just like every other business, but instead of keeping the profits they make for themselves, non-profits give it all back to help others.

Imagine creating t-shirts with fun designs and selling them to raise money for something important to you.

With this business, every dollar of profit you earn will go towards making a positive impact in your community! Don't forget the lessons we learned in Book 2 though. You still need to keep enough money to cover the costs of the business (like buying more blank t-shirts) so that you can keep it running and help even more people!

Another fantastic way to provide a positive impact to your community is through volunteering! This doesn't require you to donate any money, you just donate your time to help a cause that you believe in!

For instance, you could head to the local park and lend a hand by picking up trash. By doing this, you're showing how much you care about keeping your community clean and beautiful!

Now that we know how to make a positive impact in our community, let's discover why it's important to do so!

One of the best reasons is the happiness and pride we feel when we make our community a better place.

When we help other people and animals, or clean up the land, we can see the immediate impact we have on our community.

For example, it's an amazing feeling to see how beautiful a local forest becomes after we pick up the trash.

While you're providing a positive impact on your community, you're also getting practice using important skills! And you could be learning new ones!

Maybe you decide to start the t-shirt non-profit that we discussed earlier in the chapter. You can practice your sales skills when selling the shirt!

Or maybe you would prefer to do more volunteering. You can gain experience with leadership skills while getting your friends together to clean the park!

It's important to remember that learning new skills, and practicing things that we already know, is something we're always doing. Sometimes we just need to recognize it!

Once you discover how amazing it feels to make a positive difference in your community, you won't want to stop! Your hard work and effort can make your neighborhood a better place to live. Keep going, and one day you'll see your area become even more wonderful than it already is!

"The more you read, the more things you know.

The more that you learn, the more places you'll go."

-Dr. Seuss

Chapter 2:

Exploring New Horizons:

Investing in Education and Learning

For Parents

Key Themes Explored in this chapter:

- This chapter focuses on the importance of continuous education. We specifically do not discuss college vs trade schools or any other higher education platforms. Instead, our hope is to focus on the importance of education outside of a curriculum and done by reading books, listening to podcasts, watching educational videos, or any other medium where we learn new ideas.

- Throughout the chapter we show options for investing your time and money into education, like taking courses from experts in a field that you are interested in.

- We conclude by showing that life-long learning is a skill that can take you anywhere!

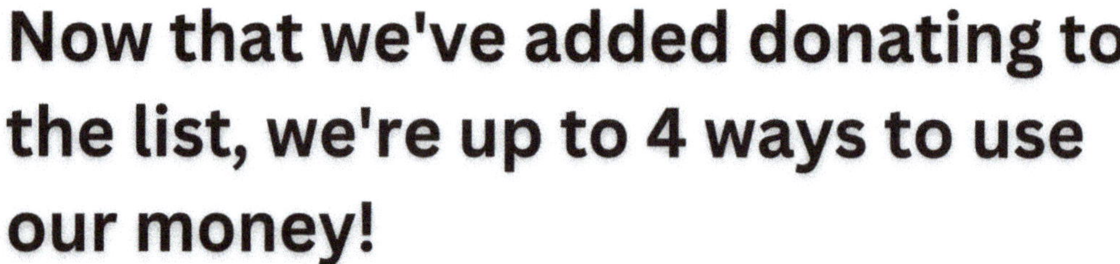

Now that we've added donating to the list, we're up to 4 ways to use our money!

1) Spending it on things we want or need.

2) Saving it for later.

3) Investing it to make more money.

4) Donating it to charities or other good causes!

In this chapter we'll explore a 5th way to use our money. Investing it in ourselves through education!

Investing in education is all about using our resources to learn and grow.

When we invested in our lemonade stand, we used the money to buy lemons and sugar. Those things aren't worth very much on their own, but when you combine them together they become more valuable...as lemonade!

We can also do the same thing with ourselves and education by investing in learning new knowledge and skills!

It's like discovering a magical door that opens up a world of possibilities!

For instance, investing in this book and learning from it can help us unlock new knowledge about personal finances and expand our horizons for the future!

There are many ways to invest in your education! Many of them don't cost any money, they just cost you some of your time!

But sometimes there are specific classes that we want to take which do cost money.

Just like buying a toy, we can use some of our money to sign-up for exciting courses that teach us new things. It's like having a treasure chest full of knowledge!

On the next page we'll see an example! But remember, when you decide to pay for a class you need to make sure that it's worthwhile and not a waste of money! And make sure you ask a parent or guardian first before spending any money!

Some of the best classes to take are taught by people who are experts in their field!

Remember your friend who started a lawn mowing business? What if they offered a special class on how to become a lawn mowing expert like them? By taking their course, you can learn how to mow the best lawns in town and start your very own business!

If you're interested in learning about specific new skills, investing in a course about those skills is a great option!

Like we talked about at the beginning of the chapter, investing in education doesn't always mean spending money.

There are many free education tools available to you today!

Exploring libraries, reading books, and discovering information online (with your parent's help) are like planting seeds of knowledge that grow and blossom over time!

There's many types of skills that you can learn that will help you achieve different types of goals!

If you don't know where to start, investing in digital skills might be a great choice!

Learning how to navigate the internet safely, the basics of coding, and learning how to use technology responsibly can open doors to exciting opportunities and future careers.

And the best part is, you can learn these skills for free! You can then use what you learned to do almost anything you want, including make money!

Something interesting happens as we invest in our own education. We become life-long learners and explorers!

We are able to gain new skills and discover our passions. We become more confident in ourselves and gain a better understanding of the world around us.

Being educated is like having a super power! Education unlocks doors that lead to a bright future for ourselves, and for all the people we help along the way!

Maybe your education journey will end up with a spaceship ride to a distant planet!

We've learned about bringing value to your community and we've learned about providing a positive impact on your community.

Constant learning and education is the best way to figure out how to do these things!

Whether your goal is to learn how to make a few extra dollars a week, or your goal is to one day explore far-off planets for humanity, education is the key to your success!

"The best time to plant a tree was 20 years ago.

The second best time is now."

- Chinese Proverb

Chapter 3:

From Little Seeds to Great Fortunes:

The Magic of Long Term Investing

For Parents

Key Themes Explored in this chapter:

- In this chapter, we dive into the importance of long-term investing and how it plays a crucial role in building future wealth. We illustrate this concept by taking a close look at a small apple seed, which represents an initial investment. Over time, we witness the transformation of this seed into a magnificent orchard, just like an investment portfolio would grow over time.

- We explore the concept of compound interest by observing the growth of the first apple tree as it matures and starts producing its own apples. These apples, in turn, have the potential to become new apple trees. This process showcases the power of compound interest, which exhibits an exponential yield curve over time.

- Activity to Try at Home!: Engage your child in a fun experiment to demonstrate the concept of compound interest and its exponential growth. Offer them a small piece of candy today and present them with the choice to wait a week to receive two pieces of candy instead. If they choose to wait then give them the choice to take two pieces of candy the next week or offer them the option to wait another week for four pieces of candy. Repeat this activity to illustrate how patience and delayed gratification can lead to significant rewards over time, just like the power of compound interest. This hands-on experience will help them understand the concept in a real-life context.

We've learned a lot in this book series so far! In the last chapter we added continuing education to our list of things we can do with money (and our time!). Let's look at the list now!

1) Spend our money

2) Save our money

3) Invest our money

4) Invest our money and time in our community

5) Invest our money and time into our continued learning and education

Besides #1 spending our money, do you know what the rest of these items on the list have in common?

The more time we give them to grow, the better they become! Just like growing a big tree!

Throughout this chapter we're going to learn about one of the most important concepts in the world when it comes to making money! It's called Compound Interest! We'll use an analogy to explain it over the next few pages.

Let's think about an apple. The apple is worth just a few dollars.

Right now we might only have one apple, but in the future we'd like to have a whole apple orchard!

If we want to make that happen, the first thing we'll need to do is plant the apple!

Just like starting with a small apple to grow an apple tree, we began our money-growing adventure by saving our spare change in the magical piggy bank we learned about in Book 1!

For our apple to turn into a tree, all it really needs is time!

To help the apple grow faster though we give it extra water and fertilizer. We should water our apple on a regular basis to help it grow big and strong!

Think of the water and fertilizer that we give to our apple like it's the money that we save every week from adding value to our community! We add these savings to our magic piggy bank just like we water the apple while it turns into a tree!

As our savings grow bigger we can turn them into investments, just like we did with our class in Book 2!

You have two options when it comes to watering your tree. You can use a watering can and do it yourself, or you can set up a special sprinkler system that does it automatically!

Just like the sprinkler system takes care of watering the tree without you needing to think about it, setting up your investments to happen automatically is the best way to let them grow over time!

One of the easiest ways to do this is to always put a certain percent of the money you make into investments! For example, every time you make $5, you could put $1 into your investment! This would be saving 20%, a great goal!

As we keep watering our apple tree, something magical happens. It grows bigger and stronger, and before we know it, it starts to produce its very own apples! This is when the real excitement of growing an apple orchard, and investing, begins!

Remember how we said each apple was worth a few dollars. And we said the money we make from adding value goes into watering the tree.

So these new apples are dollars that have been created just by investing our money! Without any real work from us at all other than putting our money away into investments!

We touched on this in Book 2 when we received our money back from the teacher and it was $6 instead of the $5 we invested at the beginning. We'll discuss this again later in the chapter!

Now that our tree has apples, we have a decision to make! Do we take apples off the tree and eat them ourselves, or do we plant the apples and grow more trees?

Compound interest begins when we take those new apples and we plant them to grow into their own trees!

Remember at the beginning of the chapter when we said Compound Interest is extremely important? This example shows why!

If we had decided to take all the money (apples) that we had made and spent it on something else, we would be missing out on all the new trees those apples will grow into!

On the next page we'll show this with numbers so it makes some more sense!

Let's use some easy math to show how Compound Interest works.

Let's say that each apple tree produces 10 apples, and it take 1 year to grow a single tree.

At the end of the year 1, we'll have 10 new apples!

If we then go and plant all 10 of those apples, we'll have 100 new apples at the end of year 2 from the 10 new trees!

And if we plant all of those apples, we'll have 1,000 apples at the end of year 3!

You may have learned about exponents in school. Compound Interest is an example of exponential growth in real life! You can see how every year the number gets much bigger than the year before. But this only works if you re-plant the apples instead of eating them every year!

Earlier in the chapter we said that time is a key factor in the success of our investments. We saw that with the apple orchard and how it took until the 3rd year to get 1,000 apples.

Now let's look at this in a more practical example. Think back to when we invested in lemonade stands with our class in Book 2. Back then, we asked for our money back right away from our teacher.

But what if we decided to let them keep our money a little longer? Let's explore what magical things can happen when we give our money more time to grow!

Time is like a superpower when it comes to making money, just like we saw with the apple orchard!

In the class example, there were two lemonade stands that lost money because of a rainstorm. Luckily, the third one made enough money to cover their losses!

At the time, we decided to take our money out of the mutual fund by asking our teacher for it back.

If we had known how important time was for making money, we would have left our money invested with the class longer! This is because we would have known that the next weekend the sun would come back out and all three lemonade stands would make more money! Our $5 could have turned into $10 if we had let it grow long enough!

This teaches us an important lesson: being patient with our money and investments can lead to even more money in the end!

In the exciting world of investing, there's one valuable lesson to remember: small actions, given enough time, can lead to huge rewards!

It's like when we started our apple orchard with just a single apple! We then gave it just a little bit of water every time we could. Then, before we knew it, we had a whole apple orchard!

"Time is the most valuable asset you have. Invest it wisely."

-Warren Buffett

Chapter 4:

Money is Time:

Using Money to Chase our Dreams!

For Parents

Key Themes Explored in this chapter:

- In this chapter, we conclude the entire series by introducing a fresh perspective on money: money equals time. We delve into this idea by examining the process of buying an apple from the store instead of growing an apple tree from a seed. By purchasing the apple, we are essentially acquiring not just the fruit itself, but also the months of effort and labor that would have been required to grow the tree and produce the apple.

- We explore the profound impact of this simple mental shift - from using money to purchase things, to using money to buy time - and how it can grant us the freedom to pursue any dream we envision in the future. By recognizing that money is just a tool to create more time for ourselves, we open up a world of possibilities and empower ourselves to chase our dreams with a strong financial backing.

- We conclude the series with a message of hope and appreciation for the invaluable gift you, as parents, are providing to your children. By teaching them financial literacy from a young age, you are equipping them with the tools and knowledge to accomplish their goals and navigate their financial future with confidence. Your dedication to their financial education is an investment that will yield lifelong benefits and set them on a path towards financial independence and success.

The very first thing we learned in this series was that money can be used to buy the things we want or need.

This is still true, but maybe it's a pretty basic understanding of money?

What if instead of thinking about money as a way to buy "things", we instead think of money as a way to buy time?

You might hear the phrase "time is money" said; however the reverse is actually true. We'll learn more about this over the next few pages!

Imagine you really want a fresh apple. You have two options to get that apple.

You can either go to the grocery store and spend $1.50 to get an apple.

Or you can go to the store and spend $0.10 to get an apple seed, that you would then grow into a tree over the course of a very long time!

This is clearly an analogy, but simple stories like this help us think about money as a tool for buying time! Instead of taking a year to grow an apple, you spent $1.50 to have the apple today!

Here's where things get interesting!

When we start to see money as time, it completely changes the way we do things in life, and it can lead to some really cool outcomes!

To begin with, you might notice yourself asking questions like "is that new toy worth spending an hour to mow the lawn for?" Whereas before you may have asked if the toy is worth spending $5 on, but now you may begin to see that you're spending time instead of money.

As you get older your mindset might shift again. Maybe in the future you'll think, "mowing the lawn takes an hour and I could make $5 doing it, or I could spend $5 and have someone else mow the lawn while I do something that I enjoy more."

The more money we have and the more money we make, the more we start to see that money is just a tool that lets us buy time and freedom!

Remember the apple trees from the last chapter? We showed how one little apple turned into a whole orchard.

Once you've built up that orchard you'll have the ability to spend your time doing whatever you want!

Keep in mind that it's crucial that you don't start spending too much of your money on purely fun things too early in your life! Remember in the apple tree example how every tree produced 10 apples?

Now imagine that instead of re-planting those apples (so that you could get 10 new trees), you ate 9 of the apples instead! How much longer do you think it would take to get to 1,000 apples if you only re-planted 1 a year? It might be impossible!

Spending too much money can have the same affect on your future orchard!

Let's do a small activity and take the next few pages to imagine our future lives and what we want to be when we grow up!

Maybe you want to be a video game streamer? Sharing how much fun playing different games is with your audience?

It's important to dream big about our futures and to not stop dreaming when we grow up!

Dreaming about our future gives us a goal to reach. Sometimes the goals help us grow our orchard, but sometimes we realize that we need to grow our orchard in other ways so that we can complete our goals in the future!

Maybe you've been inspired to want to be a Firefighter when you grow up!

Being a Firefighter means you can provide value to your community, because you get paid a salary.

But you can also provide a positive impact on your community as you help people on their worst days!

Being a Firefighter is a very honorable and noble role in the community, but even Firefighters need to make sure they're saving and investing their money so that their orchard is always growing!

Maybe you've been inspired to visit the stars by NASA's Artemis mission? Exploring the final frontier on the Moon or Mars as an astronaut certainly sounds exciting!

Even while in space, your apples down on earth can still be growing into an orchard for you! That way when you come home you won't have to worry about having enough money!

But if you don't plant that first apple in the ground and continue to water it, your orchard will never begin to grow!

No matter what you decide to do when you grow up, you will be awesome at it!

But here's the last lesson: knowing about money can make your life even more enjoyable.

When you understand how money works and how to manage it wisely, you won't have to worry about not having enough. That way, you can focus on doing what you love and being happy in your chosen career!

Congratulations! You've completed the entire book series!

Hopefully, you gained valuable knowledge about personal finances and how to think about money!

Remember, what you've learned will stay with you forever. By making wise choices with your money and time, you can create an amazing future for yourself.

Keep exploring, keep learning, and make the most of every moment. Your future is filled with endless possibilities, and you have the power to make it bright and successful!

About the Authors

Nick and Ben embarked on the journey of creating the "My First Financial Literacy Book" series because they had witnessed firsthand the challenges faced by young adults in managing their finances and the overwhelming stress caused by a lack of financial literacy. As young Officers in the U.S. Army, they often found themselves consoling fellow Soldiers who had lost all their money due to a lack of understanding about personal finances. On multiple occasions, they found themselves confronting predatory payday lenders on behalf of their Soldiers. It was clear to them that if these 18-year-old individuals targeted by such lenders were financially literate, they would have been able to avoid the need for these types of loans. Even after transitioning into the civilian world, they continue to observe these same mistakes repeating themselves, with some taking over two decades to rectify.

"It is our mission to empower future generations by equipping them with essential financial knowledge, and we sincerely appreciate your support on this Financial Literacy journey!" - Nick and Ben